THE DRUMMER GIRL
coloring book

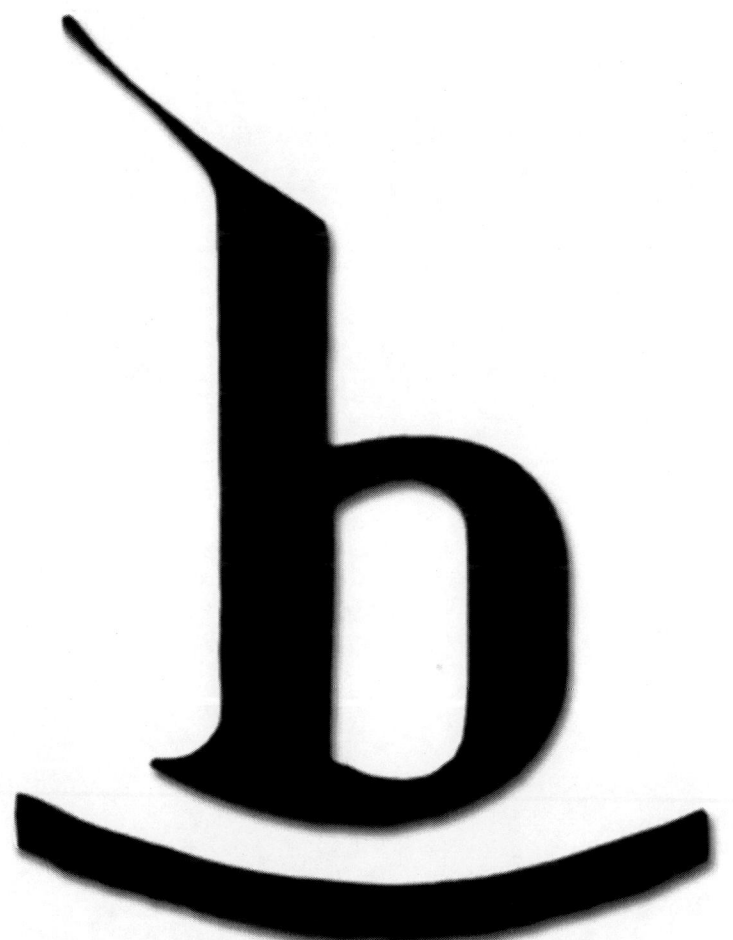

The Brittany Brand

www.thebrittanybrandco.com

Copyright © 2017 Brittany Brooks

The Brittany Brand Publishing

All rights reserved.

ISBN-13: 978-1542772310

ISBN-10: 1542772311

I dedicate this passion project of mine to God!
I realize and humbly acknowledge that without His grace I wouldn't have this gift
nor the opportunity to share it!
Proverbs 18:16

I was just a child when I started playing the drums. I had no idea of the
Possibilities that existed out there. I just wanted to play!
I practiced everyday. All I talked about was drums. I dreamt about it, I wrote about it
In my journal, I studied the greats and eventually my goals and aspirations were beginning to form.
Once I saw what was possible, I went full speed into my passion.
Write it out, make it plain, and get to work!
There is power behind a well planned vision!

If I have never said it before,
Thank You Mom and Dad
for being the first to believe in me!
Oh, and letting me turn half of your garage into my
personal drum practice room!

Brittany walked into her 6th grade beginning band class excited to learn how to play an instrument!

The drums caught her eye right away and there was no doubt that the drums were Brittanys number one choice!

When the teacher asked Brittany what instrument she wanted to play, she immediately blurted out **"DRUMS"** and that was the birth of a dream!

From there on out, Brittany was known as

"The Drummer Girl"

Brittanys passion for playing the drums came long before her skills developed. Everywhere she went, she had a pair of drumsticks in her hands.

Friends, family and neighbors were always very supportive of Brittany wanting to play drums.

Every chance she got, she loved to show her friends at schoot something new she learned in class. She would play on anything, a table, a trash can, a tree trunk, or even a friends backpack.

She loved her new hobby so much and she made sure everyone around her knew it!

Brittanys bed was often the home of sprawled out handwritten charts.
She could sit in her room for hours drawing out music charts and notating drum parts.

She would often take a break to write in her journal.

Brittany had big dreams even from the beginning and would often journal about one day becoming a professional drummer and traveling the world playing drums in front of thousands of people!

Brittany became a regular at her local drum shop! She would go there and play on the drums in the shop.

Sometimes customers would gather around and watch as Brittany would practice her favorite beats she learned in class.

She loved playing the drums so much and coming to The Drum World every weekend helped her stay prepared for class on Monday mornings!

Brittany showed her parents that she was really dedicated to playing the drums. So on one special day, Brittany came home from school to a big surprise!

Her parents bought her a shiny new drumset of her own!

Brittany was so excited!

Brittany and her drumset were inseparable!

She practiced everyday after school for hours. Sometimes until late in the evening.

With all that practice, Brittany was becoming a great drummer!

In school, the music teacher would have Brittany draw out charts with drum rudiments and paradiddles to practice for homework.

These exercises would help Brittany build speed and strength on the drumset.

Test is on Friday!

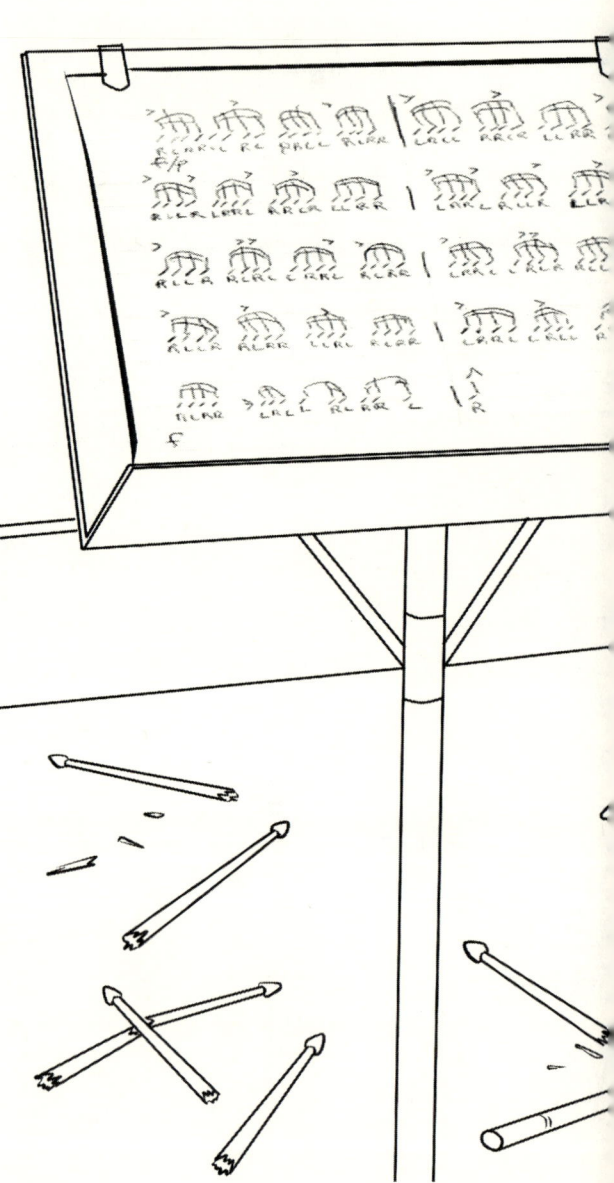

She had dreams about playing the drums in front of large crowds!

At the end of the school year, the music department held a concert in the school gymnasium.

This was Brittanys first time playing the drums in front of a big crowd!

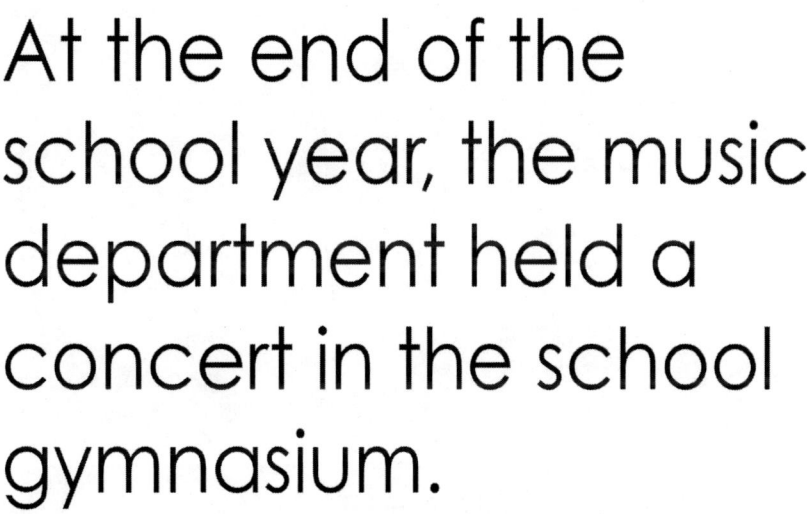

When Brittany went to high school, she joined the schools marching band!

She played the snare drum in the drumline.

This is where she learned how to do fancy stick twirls and tricks!

But she kept her evening routine of practicing on her drumset. She even started applying some of her stick tricks to the drumset!

Brittany graduated from high school and was excited about her next big chapter in her young life!

She knew that if she was going to reach her childhood dreams than it was time to put her plan into action and take some big steps!

And with the help of her parents, she packed up everything she owned and moved to Los Angeles to begin a new chapter in her life.

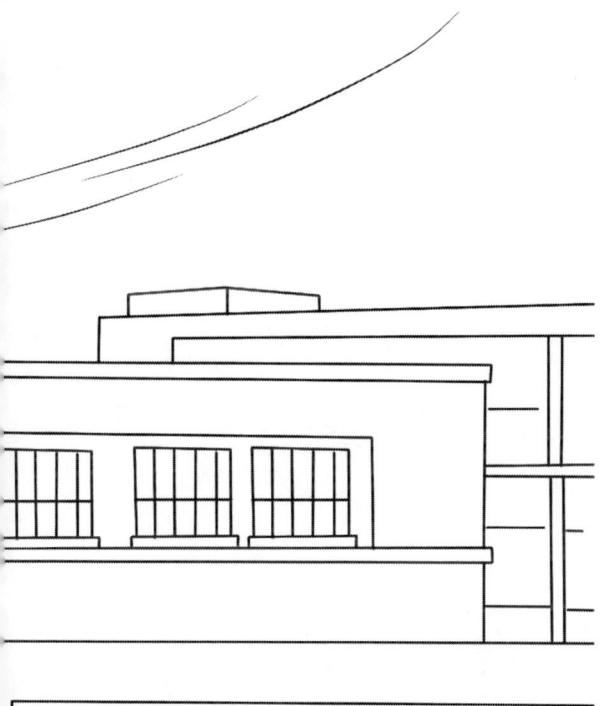

Brittany enrolled as a full time music student. She took drum classes all day and in the evenings she would go listen to local bands.

She met many people and quickly became the "New Girl Drummer" in town.

Brittany was pretty well adjusted to her new life in LA and after a while, she started going on auditions!

One day, there was an audition being held for a big singer that was putting together a band for his upcoming international tour.

Brittany went to the audition and she did so well that she was hired on the spot!

Brittany got her very first professional job as a drummer!

Within weeks she was boarding her first international flight to go on tour.

All of her hard work was beginning to pay off!

One evening, Brittanys family was back home gathered around the television watching Brittany playing the drums for the first time on tv!

They were all so proud of her accomplishments!

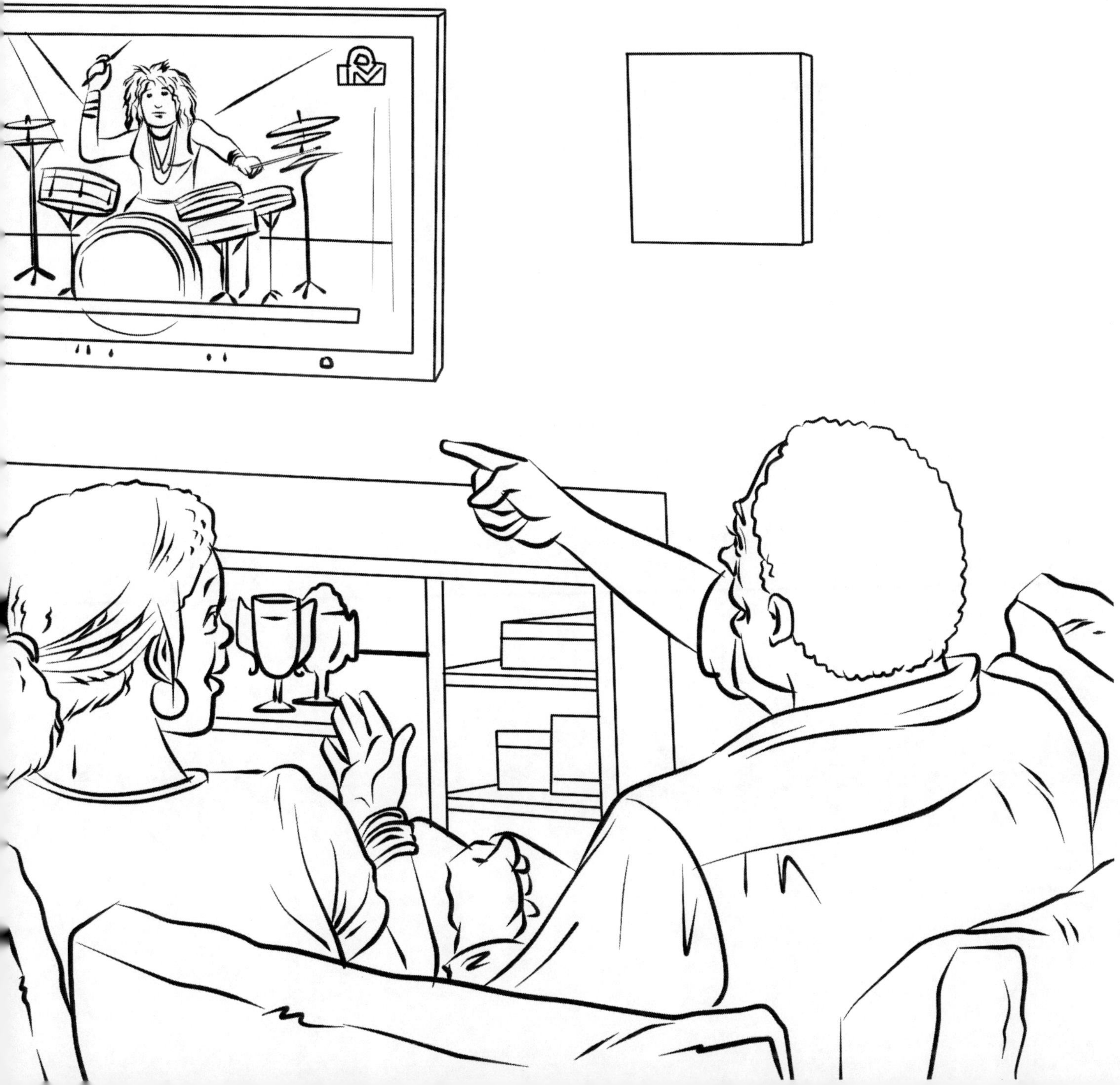

Soon after, Brittany was given the opportunity to design her very own signature shoe for a company that makes shoes for drummers!

She helped the company develop the womens line!

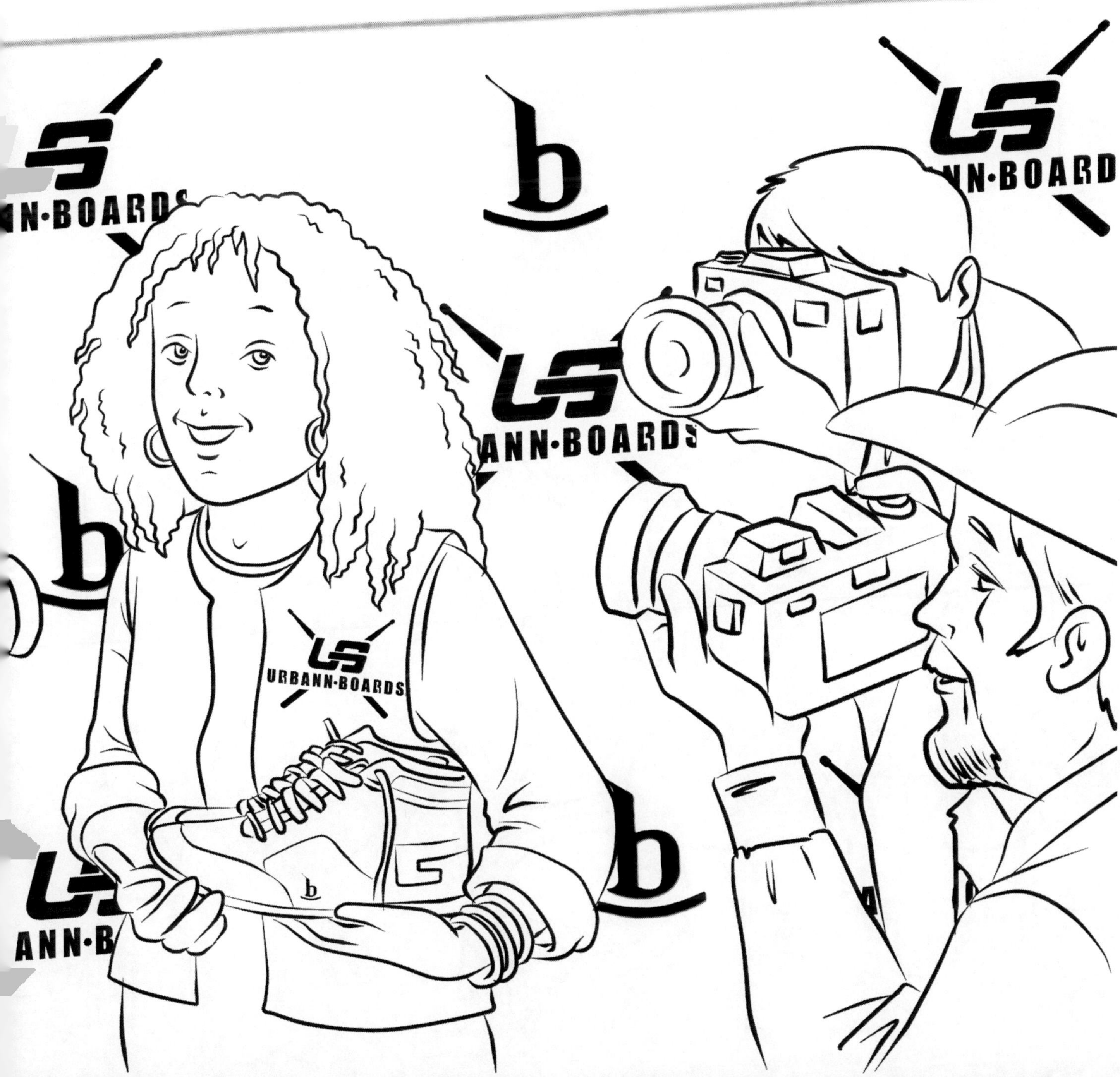

N·BOARDS
ANN·BOARDS
URBANN·BOARDS
NN·BOARD
ANN·B

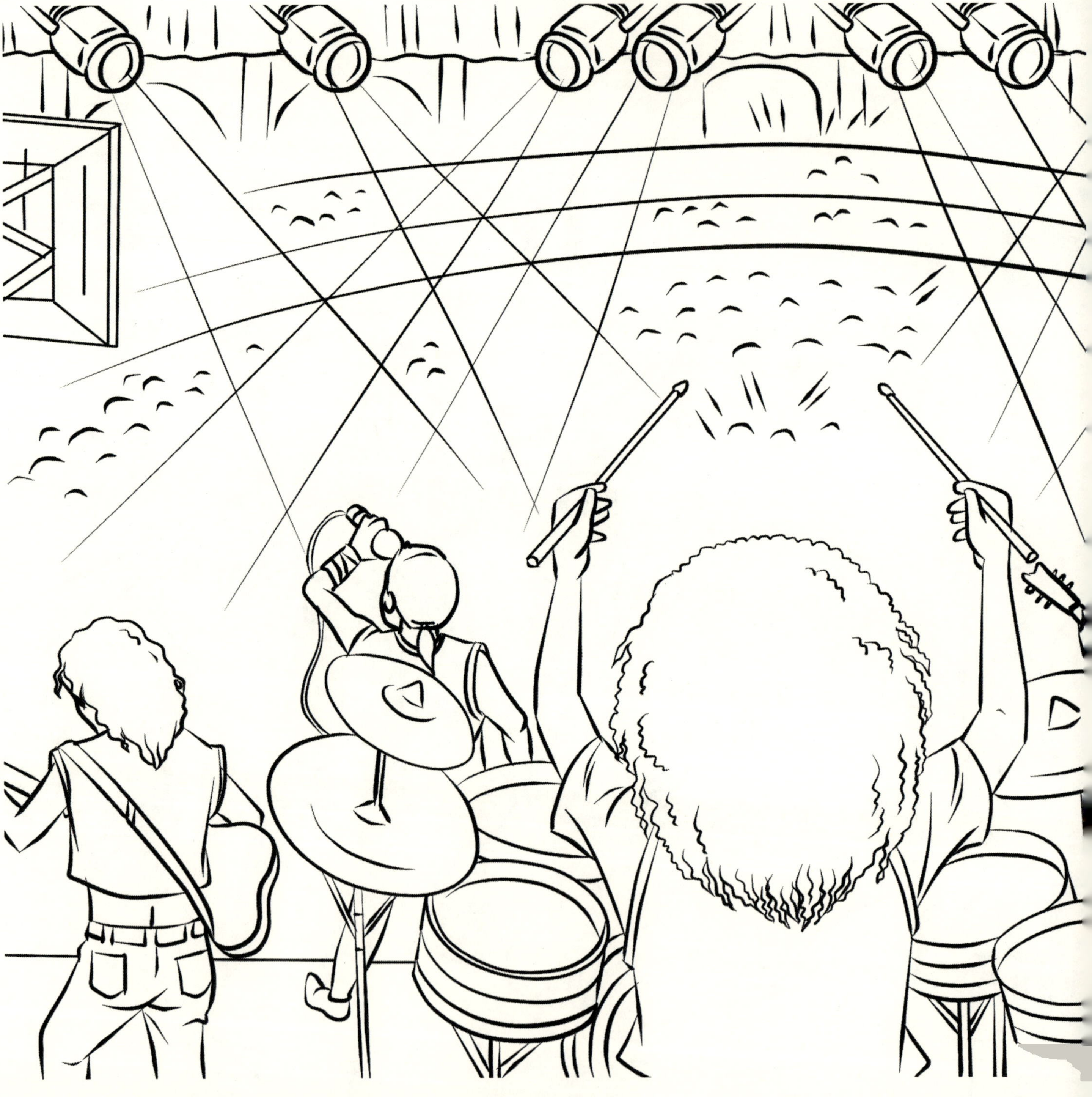

She did it!
As a child, Brittany wanted to be able to travel the world and play the drums for thousands of people.

She worked hard everyday and because of her hard work and dedication, she acheived her dreams!

THE DRUMMER GIRL
coloring book

The Brittany Brand

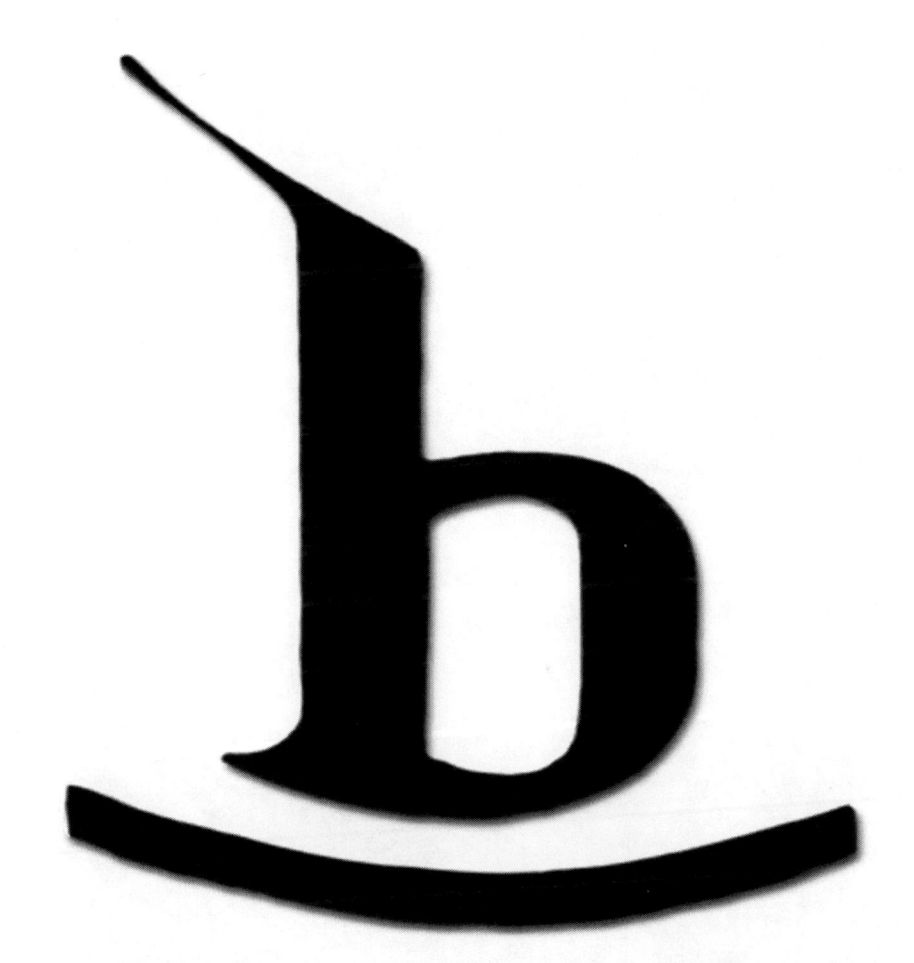

www.thebrittanybrandco.com

Made in United States
North Haven, CT
18 November 2023